W9-ALT-985

DECADES

The
EIGHTIES

Edward Grey

STECK-VAUGHN
LIBRARY
Austin, Texas

DECADES

The Fifties
The Sixties
The Seventies
The Eighties

**Published in the United States in 1990
by Steck-Vaughn Co., Austin, Texas,**
a subsidiary of National Education Corporation

First published in 1989 by Wayland (Publishers) Ltd
© Copyright 1989 Wayland (Publishers) Ltd

Edited by Roger Coote
Designed by Helen White

Series Consultant: Stuart Laing
Dean of Cultural and Community Studies
University of Sussex

Consultant, American Edition: Jack Nelson
Graduate School of Education
Rutgers University

Library of Congress Cataloging-in-Publication Data

Grey, Edward, 1949-
 The eighties / Edward Grey.
  p. cm.—(Decades)
 "First published in 1989 by Wayland (Publishers) Ltd."—T.P.
verso.
 Includes bibliographical references.
 Summary: Discusses the youth culture of the eighties, highlighted
by fitness, Michael Jackson, Dungeons and Dragons, breakdancing,
AIDS, and politically by the first flight of the space shuttle and
Gorbachev's assumption of power in the Soviet Union.
 ISBN 0-8114-4215-2
 1. United States—History—1969- —Juvenile literature. 2. United
States—Popular culture—History—20th century—Juvenile literature.
3. United States—Social life and customs—1971- —Juvenile
literature. 4. History, Modern—1945- —Juvenile literature.
5. Popular culture—History—20th century—Juvenile literature.
(1. Popular culture—History—20th century. 2. History,
Modern—1945-) I. Title. II. Series.
E839.G73 1990   89-27178
909.82'8—dc20   CIP
                                                     AC

Typeset by Multifacit Graphics, Keyport, NJ
Printed by G. Canale, C.S.p.A., Turin, Italy
Bound by Lake Book, Melrose Park, IL.

1 2 3 4 5 6 7 8 9 0 Ca 94 93 92 91 90

Contents

INTRODUCTION

In times of hardship people often turn to established customs and values for reassurance. In a sense, that was what happened in the 1980s. The decade began amid a business slump and widespread unemployment. These brought conservative politicians to the fore: in the United States Ronald Reagan was president from 1981 to 1989, and in Britain Margaret Thatcher was prime minister throughout the entire decade. The two leaders shared similar ideas. Both stressed the importance of hard work, individual effort, and family values in a nation's life. They tended to be unsympathetic toward people who expected the government to solve their problems for them. And they placed great emphasis on national pride.

Permissiveness, the idea that young people should be free to do as they please, had started to go out of fashion in the seventies. During the eighties this trend accelerated. In the United States there was a return to traditional religious faith through such activities as the Born-again

Above *Soviet premier Mikhail Gorbachev and President Ronald Reagan embrace after concluding a historic arms agreement in 1987.*

Christian movement. And everywhere the rapid spread of the alarming new disease of AIDS made people more cautious about casual sex.

All of this meant that young people were not as rebellious as those of the sixties generation had been. Those who found a job or whose parents were working might expect a comfortable life, with many exciting new electronic entertainment products available, such as videos, computer games, personal stereos, and compact disc (CD) players. Some teenagers facing unemployment and poverty, however, experienced real despair. Heroin, cocaine, and crack addiction created serious problems among young people.

The threat of nuclear war was also a cause for concern. During much of the decade there was great rivalry between the United States

Below *A Japanese poster warns against AIDS. The disease cannot be transmitted simply by kissing, but it did make teenagers more cautious about sex.*

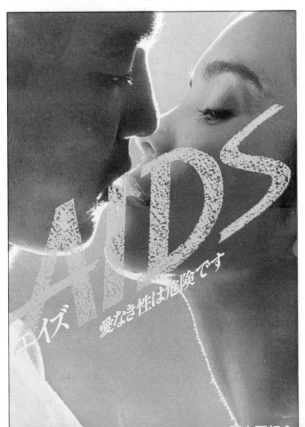

and the Soviet Union. Tensions ran so high that the United States refused to attend the 1980 Olympic Games in Moscow, and the Soviets refused to attend the Olympics held four years later in Los Angeles. In 1985, however, Mikhail Gorbachev came to power in the Soviet Union. His policies brought a greater degree of democracy and openness to his country, and helped to ease tensions with the United States. In 1987, the two superpowers signed a major arms agreement. Their continuing dialogue was a great cause for optimism.

Teenagers did campaign widely for nuclear disarmament. But they did not quite have the prominence in society that young people in the sixties had enjoyed. It is often said that teenage culture fragmented, or broke up, in the seventies and the eighties. No single movement caught people's imagination in the way that the hippies had done in the sixties. Instead, there was a host of small cultures. Youth cultures ranged from the conservative youngsters known as "preppies" to fans of the tough rap music that came out of the black ghettoes. The various groups had little in common with one another and did not have a sense of mission that joined them like the hippies.

Youth culture did not die out, however—it had simply become much more varied. Worldwide, the music and fashion industries catered to a wealth of different tastes and there were many positive signs for the future. One of these was the rise of global rock concerts, held to raise money for charity. At the famous Live Aid event of 1985 pop stars from all over the world came together for a concert that raised over $70 million for famine relief in Ethiopia. Live Aid was watched by 1.5 billion people in 160 countries, all linked by satellite communications. Members of the younger generation were taking on large responsibilities, and helping to bind people together throughout the world.

FASHION

During the seventies punk rockers had created a harsh sort of anti-fashion by wearing ripped clothes, zipper fasteners, and safety pins.

There were also many revivals of past styles, such as mens' suits from the fifties and the miniskirt from the sixties. Punk styles themselves never died out entirely but they had lost the raw power to shock. Mohican haircuts dyed in bright colors had become an ornamental fashion device for many.

In the early eighties a handful of young trendsetters brought back a taste for glamour

Above *"New Romantics" photographed in King's Road, Chelsea, England. This area had long been a center for youth fashions.*

and fantasy in clothing. They were nicknamed the New Romantics and they took delight in dressing up; whether as pirates, highwaymen, matadors, or gypsies. Frilly shirts, satin knickers and sashes were all part of the look that had some influence on fashions in the early part of the decade in English cities.

Classic style

Probably the most surprising teenage trend, however, was the return to the cool, traditional look of expensive adult clothing. People first noticed what was happening in the United States where the "preppy look" spread in 1980–81. For years fashionable youngsters had been wearing bizarre styles to stand out from the adult world. Now, they seemed to want to join that world, copying the traditional styles that well-to-do young prep school students (or "preppies") had been wearing for years. This clothing, which came close to being a uniform, included navy blue blazers, Shetland sweaters, and white-soled boating shoes known as "topsiders." Polo shirts with distinctive emblems and logos were also typical.

The *Official Preppy Handbook*, a humorous look at the style, gave step-by-step instructions to would-be preppies. It became a bestseller and the trend inspired a similar craze in Britain. People started to copy the type of clothing worn by so-called Sloane Rangers, public-school types who owed their nickname to the residential area around Sloane Square in London. The Barbour, a weatherproof waxed jacket worn by "Sloanes" in the country, became a very fashionable item. And fascination with upper-class style was increased through the media attention given to Prince Charles's young fiancée Lady Diana Spencer. The couple married in 1981, and "Princess Di" became a fashion symbol for many young women worldwide.

Designer labels

With this sophisticated trend came a craze for "designer labels" on clothing. Clothes conspicuously bearing the labels and logos of

Below Classic style. *This American model displays the smooth, sophisticated, traditional look favored by many young men in the eighties. Note the tailored waist and padded shoulders.*

Below *A youth models Levis 501s. The look recalls the fifties, but the mass of jacket badges was an eighties fashion.*

pricey designers became desirable, partly because it suggested a rich and privileged lifestyle. American designers such as Calvin Klein and Ralph Lauren created especially elegant, relaxed clothes based on traditional jackets, slacks, skirts, and shirts. Liz Claiborne, Esprit, and Guess were three other popular labels to be seen wearing.

Throughout the eighties people showed an increasing passion for health and fitness, and many items of sportswear such as track suits, cycling shorts, and sneakers became fashionable as casual wear. They were created for slim, lean bodies and the labels again carried a lot of importance. Many teenagers felt that their sneakers *had* to be made by Nike, Adidas, or Reebok.

Inexpensive denim jeans had long been standard wear for teenagers around the world but they went out of fashion in the early eighties. If jeans were worn at all they had to have a designer label and unique features—or be authentic Levis 501s.

Flat tops and designer stubble

Male teenagers tended to wear their hair short and neat in the eighties. One of the most distinctive styles of the time was the "flat top" or wedge, which looked very much as the names suggest. The hair was shaved very close at the sides and stood up in a perfectly straight wedge of bristles on top. In some ways it recalled the crew cuts of servicemen, but the most extreme examples were so geometric that they gave people's heads a futuristic, robot look. Designers of the time were fascinated with advanced technology; the flat top was a "high-tech" hairstyle. Blunt layers over short hair underneath gave longer hair a geometric look, too.

Older teenagers liked to visit nightclubs and cocktail bars where jazz music experienced a big revival. For the smooth, sophisti-

Above Cool, relaxed clothes designed by Ralph Lauren.
The masculine style of the woman's clothes reflects
changing attitudes to women in society.

Above *A flat-top haircut worn here with a white turtle-neck. Notice the earring, an accessory often adopted by male teenagers in the late eighties.*

cated look, young men might wear a black turtleneck sweater. Black remained fashionable for both sexes during the decade.

As with all trends, the clean-cut look began to lose its appeal as time passed, and young men started to cultivate a rougher appearance. One fad was for stylish young men to go about unshaven—it was said that they had "designer stubble." This look was also sported by Don Johnson of TV's *Miami Vice*. Designer jeans were sold deliberately torn, and the style even reached local department stores.

Female style

Teenage girls also reacted against too sophisticated a style. In the mid-eighties, for example, pop star Madonna created a deliberately trashy look that included black lingerie worn with beads, crucifixes, and heavy makeup. This look quickly caught on with some teenage girls. Some feminists objected to the style, believing that it created a negative stereotype and a return to old-fashioned ways of looking at women as mere playthings for men. However, others

saw it as an expression of young women's new confidence in themselves; girls could wear what they pleased without feeling embarrassed or threatened.

In general, clothing styles for older, working women had become increasingly masculine as women made up about half of the work force. Most women wore dark, tailored suits and high-necked blouses. As the decade progressed, however, women's business fashions became more feminine but still suitable for the work-place. The eighties were a time for variety. Every young woman was free to put together her own look according to her taste or mood. And some very mixed styles emerged. For example, a young woman might wear a short, flouncy skirt—but with men's oxford shoes. The footwear was a comment on the skirt, and showed the girl was in control of her image.

Below *Beads, bangles, and black lace made the look of pop star Madonna, who had a string of hit singles in the eighties.*

POP MUSIC

I n July 1985 some of the world's best-known rock stars took part in a marathon concert to raise money for famine victims in Ethiopia. Called the Live Aid concert, some stars performed at Wembley stadium in London; others at John F. Kennedy stadium in Philadelphia. The 16-hour event was beamed around the world by satellite and seen by millions on television. Apart from the huge sums of money raised, it showed the enormous importance that rock music now played in peoples' lives. It had become a global form of entertainment, not only for teenagers but for whole families.

Above Annie Lennox and Dave Stewart of the Eurythmics had more top ten hits than any other male/female duo in pop history.

Above *Paul McCartney, Bono (of U2), and George Michael performing in the Live Aid concert in England in 1985.*

Many other concerts were held to aid worthwhile causes, and records were released to raise money for charity. Rock stars had come to realize that their lives were significant to millions of people. Their influence could be used to try and change the world for the better by drawing attention to those in need.

New sounds

By the eighties, technology had brought a new generation of electronic instruments, such as synthesizers, drum machines, and computerized keyboards. Electronic instruments created a very clean, clear sound, sometimes known as "electro-pop," that fit in with the high-tech design ideas of the eighties. Groups such as Ultravox, the Human League, Depeche Mode, and the Eurythmics were among the first to explore the possibilities of the synthesizer sound and they produced many successful singles and albums. Synthesizers had other possibilities, too. In 1986, French composer Jean-Michel Jarre attracted a world-record audience of 1.3 million people for a concert in Houston, Texas, which combined electronic music with laser light shows.

Developments like these meant that old-fashioned drum-and-guitar groups, playing to live audiences, went out of style for a while. The pulsing, synthetic beat was particularly well suited to dance music, and synthesizer groups such as the Pet Shop Boys rarely played live, preferring to concentrate on perfecting their sound in the studio.

New electronic equipment was also used to create extraordinary mixtures of sound that might combine taped voices, electronic drum beats, and bits of music from other records. So long as it was all held together by a steady dance rhythm the possibilities were endless. *Pump Up the Volume*, a smash hit for MARRS in 1987, was an example of what was loosely termed House Music.

Another craze was rap music. This was a form of music that developed in the black ghet-toes throughout the country and involved talking in rhyme against a musical background. The style developed in dance clubs, where the performer was usually a disc jockey (DJ). The DJ or a partner might ''scratch'' a record rhythmically in time to the music. Rap's complex beat came from interweaving rhymes with strong percussion. The sounds could be very harsh, and some rap artists such as Public Enemy deliberately cultivated a cold, aggressive image. The Beastie Boys, a white teenage rap group, made headlines throughout the world by shocking audiences and the press with their behavior both on and off the stage.

Below *Rap group Public Enemy pose in berets, dark glasses, and military-style clothing. Their outfits recall the uniform of the revolutionary Black Panther movement of the sixties. "Hard Rap" artists often expressed anger and hostility in pop's rebellious tradition.*

Gender in rock

Toward the end of the eighties female rap artists such as Salt 'N' Pepa began to emerge. In fact, throughout the eighties, women were very prominent in the charts. Solo artists included Madonna, Whitney Houston, Tracey Chapman, and Suzanne Vega. Female groups such as the Go-Gos, the Bangles, and Bananarama were no longer treated as great curiosities. Women's roles in rock had traditionally been confined to singing solo or backup, but by the end of the decade women could be seen much more frequently as drummers, sax players, or guitarists in mixed-sex groups. Some very young teenage singers had chart hits too, including Debbie Gibson and Tiffany.

Artists might also play around with their gender roles. Annie Lennox of the Eurythmics, for example, sometimes appeared in a man's suit with close-cropped hair which gave her a very masculine look. At other times she might emphasize her femininity by wearing a wig and lipstick. Pop star Boy George of Culture Club played around with the same idea. In his early appearances he wore makeup and girls' skirts with his hair in long braids and ribbons. "I'm just a show off," he explained.

In the United States both Annie Lennox and Boy George had their TV appearances limited by TV executives who feared that viewers might find them offensive. But the stars' aim was not really to shock audiences. They wanted to question traditional ideas of what a man and woman ought to look like, and explore the variety of possibilities. Gay groups such as the Communards also had success on the charts, with members of the group making no secret of their homosexuality.

The musical mix

Variety was as much a theme of eighties music as it was of eighties fashion. Just as male and

Facing Page *The controversial Boy George and Culture Club shot to the top of the charts with the single Do You Really Want to Hurt Me? in 1982.*

Below *Salt N' Pepa were two of the new female rap artists who emerged toward the end of the eighties, transforming what had been a very masculine musical form.*

female performers were seen more and more playing alongside one another, so mixed-racial groups became more common. Britain's UB40 was one example, playing pop reggae. America's all-black Living Colour played heavy metal. The big charity rock concerts gave many Third World artists their first chance to play before large American and European audiences, and some established musicians were eager to experiment with as many influences as possible: anything from Yemenite songs to Bulgarian folk music, or the Latin Salsa beat, to the sound of the black townships of South Africa.

There were many nostalgic revivals, too. The superstar Prince was just one of many artists who experimented with images of sixties psychedelia. And heavy rock music made a big comeback with groups such as Bon Jovi, Def Leppard, and Australia's INXS. These groups

Above *Michael Jackson on stage in 1988. A child star in the early seventies with the vocal group, the Jackson Five, he became one of the superstars of the eighties.*

Above *Bruce Springsteen performs at Wembley Stadium in 1985, the year when his I'm on Fire/Born in the USA single was a hit worldwide. Notice the singer's face, projected on a giant video screen.*

appealed to many teenagers who preferred the noise and drama of big stadium concerts to synthetic dance music. New Jersey's Bruce Springsteen, known for his rousing concerts, had enormous success by drawing on images from the lives of ordinary, working-class people. And Ireland's U2 also promoted live music, creating a unique rock sound with a spiritual and visionary quality.

Superstars and indie groups

The most successful rock figure of the eighties was Michael Jackson. He had been a child star in the seventies and went on to create a solo career built around his remarkable singing and dancing talent. His *Thriller* album sold more than 35 million copies in the eighties, making it by far the best-selling album of all time. It was reported that Jackson had altered his face with

plastic surgery and that he used a life-prolonging oxygen tent. Such rumors only contributed to his fame.

Nevertheless, the music business experienced a slump in the eighties. Such large sums of money were spent on launching groups that the record companies became nervous about making mistakes. Occasional hit singles were not enough; the companies wanted artists who could be relied on to sell entire albums successfully for several years.

One result was the rise of small independent record companies known as "indies." They were less worried about reaching mass audiences and more willing to experiment with new, unusual acts. Probably the most respected of the indie groups was The Smiths, whose lead singer, Steven Morrissey, sang mournful songs with awkward, honest lyrics about the life of a shy teenager in rainy Manchester in the north of England. The Smiths developed an enormous cult following in both the United States and Great Britain.

Above *The Smiths lead singer Morrissey made its reputation with songs that included Heaven Knows I'm Miserable Now (1984).*

THE MEDIA

Teenage magazines helped to spread the new music and fashion ideas that were constantly emerging. But the general trend was against too much serious thinking about youth culture. People wanted sheer enjoyment. In the United States bestselling magazines included *Seventeen, Mademoiselle,* and *Teen;* in Britain, the colorful, jokey *Smash Hits* became a huge success while other popular magazines were *Mizz* and *Just Seventeen.*

Above *A punk of the eighties watching pop video.*

CDs and personal stereos

Audio equipment became much more sophisticated and more available in the eighties. In 1982 the Japanese firm of Sony launched the first compact disc (CD) players. CDs used laser technology to produce recorded sound of much higher quality and fidelity than earlier tapes and records. CD players were expensive, but they found their way into many homes nonetheless, and even into many cars. They became a kind of status symbol; that is, they implied that the owners were people who had achieved a certain level of wealth.

Personal stereos, however, had a much more direct impact on teenage life. The first, the Sony Walkman, was introduced in 1978 and during the eighties cheap copies were produced at prices that ordinary youngsters could afford. For the more well-to-do, Sony introduced a portable CD player late in the eighties. The stereo headphones probably contributed to the variety of different musical styles that flourished in the eighties. In the days when teenagers had listened chiefly to transistor radios they tended to pick up new tastes together. But with stereo headsets, young people pursued more individual interests.

Personal stereos suited the fitness craze of the eighties, since they could be worn while jogging, for example. And they also contributed to the increasing sales of cassettes: cassettes outsold record albums.

Cable and video

Cable TV also appeared in the eighties. This is a system by which TV programs are delivered to subscribers' homes by cable instead of being broadcast through the airwaves. The system was highly successful in the United States, where separate channels were set up for nonstop movies, music videos, news, sports, and so on. Most cable systems offered 10–15 channels. By 1985 almost half of all American homes were linked to the system, and MTV (the music television channel) was particularly popular with teenage viewers for keeping up with new developments in music and fashion.

In Britain and elsewhere, cable broadcasting developed much more slowly. Instead, there was a huge boom in the sale of video recorders. Roughly half of all British homes had a VCR by 1985—a higher percentage than in the United States—and the numbers kept on rising in the years that followed.

On both sides of the Atlantic the new technology changed viewing habits. People had

Above *Personal stereos became extremely popular in the eighties. Headsets suited the health craze because they could be worn when exercising.*

much greater freedom to choose their evening's entertainment. And rock videos became a crucial part of teenage culture, whether made for MTV or home cassette players. Michael Jackson's *Thriller*(1983), the title cut from his hugely successful album, was a video landmark. It was produced like a mini-feature film and made by the respected director, Jon Landis, who had directed the brilliant spoof horror film, *An American Werewolf in London* (1981).

Hit movies

One of the movies that had the most influence on young people in the eighties was *Fame* (1980). It described the progress of a group of teenagers at New York's High School for the Performing Arts. The scenes of high-energy dancing in the streets fired a new enthusiasm for modern dance, and the actors' costumes— leg warmers, leotards, and jogging pants—influenced clothing styles. Above all, the idea of young people of different races and both sexes striving fiercely for success helped to set the mood of the time. *Fame* inspired a TV series of the same name, which ran for several seasons. The theme song of the film was a big hit for vocalist Irene Cara.

Teenagers made up a vital section of the movie-going audience in the United States and a wealth of films were made especially for the youth market. One star who specialized in teenage roles was Michael J. Fox. He appeared, for

Below *The movie decade opened with a burst of enthusiasm as the cast of* Fame *(1980) danced in the streets. Songs included* Red Light, I Sing the Body Electric, *and* Fame (We're Gonna Live Forever).

example, in *Back to the Future* (1985) and *Teen Wolf* (1985). Both films mixed realistic American backgrounds with elements of science fiction and horror.

The great fantasy film of the eighties, however, was *ET, the Extra-Terrestrial* (1982) about a lovable space alien who is befriended by a small boy in a suburb of Los Angeles. Directed by Steven Spielberg, the movie broke all box office records to become the biggest money-maker of all time. A line spoken by the alien—"ET go home"—also became one of the catch-phrases of the decade.

The conservative spirit of America in the eighties, as well as its strong resurgence of national pride, was reflected in the success of the series of Rambo movies, beginning with *First Blood* (1982), in which Sylvester Stallone plays a Vietnam War veteran. The amount of violence worried many critics who also objected to the revival of "macho" heroes—strong, hard men good at fighting but not particularly bright. Another macho figure, though more humorously treated, was the hero *Crocodile Dundee* (1987). The original film and its sequel starred Paul Hogan as a manly but simple-minded Australian at large in New York City.

TV viewing

On TV, serials known as soaps, traditionally daytime television, moved to evenings and triumphed over all other forms of prime-time entertainment. *Dallas*, about an oil-rich Texas family, won gigantic audiences all around the world. In the United States alone, a record 80 million people watched one episode in November 1980, to find out who shot the villain J. R.

Ewing (played by actor Larry Hagman). *Dynasty*, another hugely successful soap, had an equally notorious villainess in Alexis, played by Joan Collins. Britain produced its own successful new soap in *EastEnders*, about life in a working-class community in the East End of London, and Australian soaps such as *Neighbours* also won surprise success on British TV. Teenage interest in these programs was high, and Kylie Minogue, a star of *Neighbours*, went on to make several hit records.

Black actors continued to make great progress overcoming their stereotyped, jivey TV image through programs such as *The Cosby*

Below *Actors Don Johnson (left) and Philip Michael Thomas (right) won world fame as the heroes of the stylish TV series Miami Vice.*

Above *The cast of Dallas celebrate the 250th episode of this hugely successful soap opera. The villain, J.R. Ewing, played by Larry Hagman, Jr., is seen in a blue shirt in the center of the picture.*

Show, a situation comedy that demonstrated that the tensions and the humor in black family life were much like those within white families. One of the most popular TV thriller series, *Miami Vice*, featured one black and one white detective. In this series great care was lavished on the heroes' designer clothes, the theme music was played on an electronic synthesizer, and hit music often appeared as background tracks. *Miami Vice* was very much a show of the eighties.

LEISURE

During the eighties exclusive dance clubs became fashionable among older teenagers and young adults, although very few average teenagers ever entered the most expensive of the clubs. However, many ordinary dance clubs deliberately cultivated a sophisticated image too and became more selective about who they would admit. Selection was usually on the basis of extreme dress.

Dance crazes of the time included breakdancing. This style developed among young blacks who might perform gymnastic feats such as back flips and head spins in mid-dance. "Body popping" was similar, but involved making jerky, robotic gestures. Both breakdancing and body popping might be performed on the sidewalk or in shopping malls as a form of street performance.

Above *Break-dancers performed in plazas and shopping arcades. The craze was promoted as an alternative to violence and drugs.*

A more short-lived craze was for so-called ''slam dancing.'' Teenagers in combat boots, Levis, and T-shirts simply slammed and piled into one another at dance clubs. Although it received a lot of coverage in the media it probably involved little more than a desire to let off steam. The fad lasted only for a brief period during 1983.

Keeping fit

The great leisure trend was toward physical fitness. Perfecting the body and improving health were the ideals of the eighties and they took many forms. People jogged, cycled, or ran marathons, for example. Aerobics became a household word; it referred to a program of physical exercises designed to speed up the breathing for a few minutes to strengthen the heart and stimulate blood circulation. Euryth-

Above *Jane Fonda leads a workout class. Keep-fit presenters appeared on TV shows and top personalities took part in marathon runs. Physical fitness was encouraged as a way of achieving self-respect, of keeping the mind as well as the body in tune.*

mics was another term (from which the famous rock group took its name); it meant interpreting music through graceful body movements. America's bestselling video cassette in the mid-eighties was film star Jane Fonda's *Workout*. Her tapes combined aerobic exercise and calisthenics, and came in levels for beginner, intermediate, and advanced workouts.

In addition to taking up physical exercise, teenagers were encouraged to avoid fatty foods, smoking, and harmful food additives. People promoted the idea of physical fitness as a form of self-respect among young people, as an alternative to gang violence—and to drugs.

Passing fads

In 1980–81 a baffling new craze swept the world. This was Rubik's Cube, a small cube puzzle invented by Hungarian Erno Rubik. The smaller cubes which made it up could be manipulated in many millions of different ways before a solution was found, and many people became obsessed with it. In fact, reasonably simple methods for solving the puzzle could be mastered with some practice. Techniques were learned during school recesses, and teenagers often found themselves more skilled with a cube than their parents.

Around the same time a board game called Dungeons and Dragons was also very popular. It had a medieval fantasy setting, special dice, and extraordinarily complicated rules. Again, teenagers developed skills that their parents could not hope to match.

Below *Rubik's cube was a worldwide craze in the early eighties. Erno Rubik, the Hungarian inventor, became a millionaire.*

One of the most popular books of the eighties was *The Secret Diary of Adrian Mole, Aged 13³/₄*, humorously describing the life of a very average teenage boy. But few books could compete for excitement with the new video games. Space Invaders and other space theme games had arrived in the late seventies. The new range in the eighties was more varied and included Pac-Man, a pie-shaped creature who had to be guided through a maze while eating up dots on the screen and trying not to get eaten itself. The craze for Pac-Man was such that teenagers could buy Pac-Man pens, Pac-Man pajamas, Pac-Man hats, and Pac-Man towels. Frogger, Donkey-Kong, and Zaxxon were other new video games. They might be played either on home computers, or in the new video arcades that opened up almost overnight in the United States, Europe, and elsewhere, often taking over from old pinball arcades. Many teenagers found intense thrills among their electronic blip-blips, their explosions, and their flashing lights. Parents and other adults often worried that the young were developing a real addiction to the game, but that did not limit their appeal.

Problems of youth culture

Much more serious problems of addiction came from drug abuse. The rising incidence of drug abuse was a very alarming trend, especially among the young. Major government campaigns were launched on television, in print, and in the schools to try and combat the spread of "crack" (a cheap, very addictive form of cocaine), and everywhere heroin had become a menace. This highly addictive drug was much more dangerous than earlier generations of drugs used by some teenagers. Unlike marijuana, for example, heroin could kill through overdose. And it was also associated with a new medical peril, AIDS.

AIDS (Acquired Immune Deficiency Syndrome) is a killer virus that was unheard of before the eighties. AIDS attacks and hampers the body's immune system—its ability to resist disease. One of the ways in which it spreads is through the blood, and thus on the needles sometimes shared by heroin users. Intravenous drug users quickly became one of the groups of people most at risk.

AIDS can also be transmitted from one person to another through sexual intercourse. Doctors advised young people against having sex with several partners, which obviously multiplied risks. More important still, doctors advised male teenagers to use condoms. These are rubber sheaths normally used to prevent pregnancy, which also offer vital protection against AIDS.

The publicity given to AIDS made many teenagers more cautious about sex than earlier

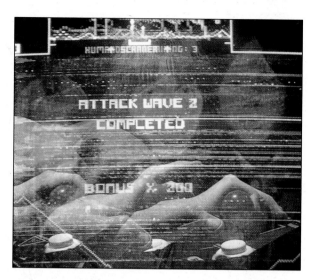

Above *The video game craze, 1981. The fascinated faces of the players can be seen reflected in the screen of this electronic game.*

Below *Teenagers reading a government pamphlet about AIDS. "Don't die of ignorance" is the message. Before the eighties AIDS was completely unknown.*

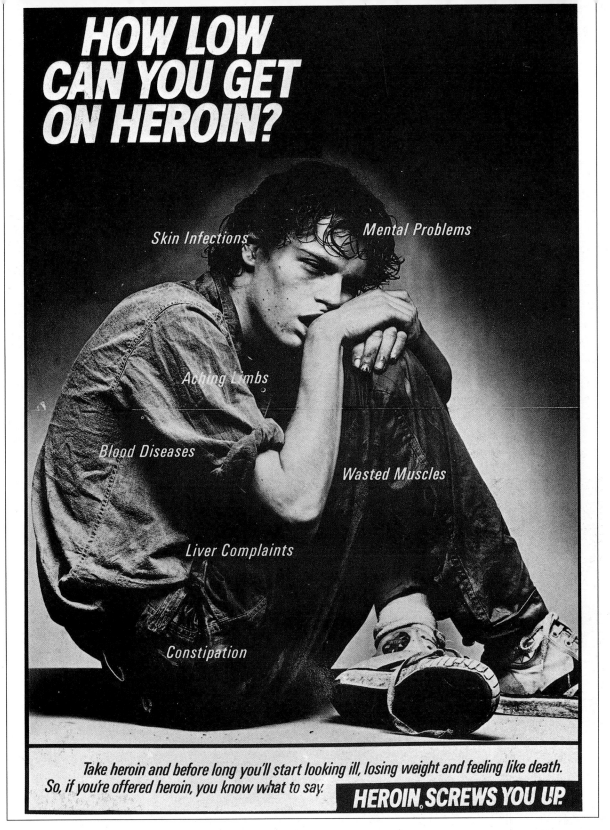

Above This British poster warns against the dangers of the highly addictive drug heroin. In the United States, the campaign against drugs had as its slogan "Just Say No."

Below *A Christian congregation at prayer in the United States. These are charismatics who believe in direct personal experience of the Holy Spirit.*

generations had been. And it may have helped to create a trend back toward the idea of choosing a single partner for life. Certainly, there was a strong reaction against permissiveness. In the United States there was a big revival of traditional moral values among Born-again Christians. These are people who have undergone an intense personal conversion to Christianity, often including the feeling of being reborn as a new person.

Born-again Christianity was a less influential movement in other countries, but Christians and others did continue to challenge permissive values. Permissive ideas were also being challenged in many Muslim countries, especially those that were undergoing a big revival of faith and stricter adherence to the Koran. In 1989 Iran's Ayatollah Khomeini ordered that the British author Salman Rushdie be killed for writing a novel, *The Satanic Verses*. Devout Muslims throughout the world believed the book to be a blasphemy against Islam, though many disputed the Ayatollah's right to order a foreign author's death without trial.

YOUTH CULTURES

In every decade since World War II, groups of teenagers have tended to form individual cultures, rather like tribes. Their clothing and musical tastes set them apart from adult society, but also from other youth cultures. There were mods and rockers in the sixties, for example, and punks and Rastafarians in the seventies. In the eighties, an extraordinary number of such tribes existed side by side rather than coming in vogue in turn. Many of them were nostalgic revivals from the past.

Above The psychedelic style, as revived in 1986. Few teenagers adopted the whole effect, but features such as floral shirts were popular.

Above *A wild black bouffon, dark lipstick, and heavy eye makeup all contribute to the look of the female Goth shown here.*

New Romantics

In England, the New Romantics wore very theatrical fashions. Some of the styles are described on page 6. The look was worn by both sexes, but the most exaggerated costumes were far too extreme to be seen much on the streets. New Romantics generally wore their finery in exclusive nightclubs.

Goths

Goths or Gothics were a new culture that emerged around the mid-eighties in England. Their style centered on all-black clothing, hair dyed jet black, and sometimes black lipstick too, all designed to emphasize pale white faces. Crucifixes might be worn also. The whole effect recalled the doom-laden zombies and vampires of horror films. Favorite groups included the Mission and the Cult.

Below *The flat top might be dyed for extra effect. It was often worn abroad with such typically American clothing as the baseball jacket seen here.*

In the late eighties many of the fashion trends were a reflection of sixties styles and colors. In music, too, several artists had big hits with remakes of sixties songs, such as "You Can't Hurry Love," originally recorded by the Supremes, and remade by Phil Collins.

Flat tops

People who wore the distinctive flat-top haircut of the eighties were often "club types." They tended to wear very fashionable clothing, usually American in style. Black blouses, shirts, and T-shirts were popular, too, and their favorite music often had a cool, jazzy sound associated with nightclubs and cocktail bars. The cover of Grace Jones' *Nightclubbing* album captures the look perfectly.

B-Boys

Fans of hip hop and rap developed a casual style of their own. The look centered around tracksuits, sneakers, and other items of sportswear, often worn with heavy gold rings on every finger and lots of gold chains and medallions. A boom box, a powerful portable radio, was part of the look.

Teddy boys and rockabillies

A number of eighties youth cultures recalled those of earlier decades. The teddy boy style that developed in Britain in the fifties was revived, for example. The men wore Edwardian-style drape jackets, shoestring ties, and hairstyles with long bangs. Women wore very full skirts. Rockabilly style also dated from the fifties and in America was built around denim jeans and jackets worn with cowboy shirts. The Confederate flag was a rockabilly emblem. The favorite music of both groups was rock'n'roll, and the rockabillies were enthusiasts of country and western music, too.

Mods and rudies

The original mods dated back to the sixties and created their style around fashionable Italian suits, neatly styled hair, parkas, and motor scooters. Mod girls wore pencil skirts and pale lipstick with a lot of eyeshadow. The rudie look was based on the two-tone suits and pork-pie hats worn by Britain's first generation Afro-Caribbeans. Both mods and rudies enjoyed Jamaican ska music, and groups such as Madness and the Specials won cult following in America and huge successes in Britain in the early eighties by combining mod and rudie styles.

Below *B-boy style was very informal and combined the two eighties crazes for rap music and sportswear. Note the boom box.*

Skinheads

The original look emerged among British teenagers around 1969. Male skinheads wore closely cropped hair, polo-type shirts, suspenders, and boots. Female skinheads wore the same type of clothes. The style was built around the idea of looking "hard" or aggressive. By the eighties skinheads had become closely associated with right-wing views and racial violence on both sides of the Atlantic.

Punk rockers

Punk rockers emerged around 1976 wearing clothing deliberately designed to shock: for example, ripped leather pants and jackets with studs, chains, zippers, and safety pins as fashion accessories. Weird hairstyles were created, sometimes in day-glo colors, dyed with leopardskin patterning, or with a Mohican cut. Favorite punk groups included the Sex Pistols and the Clash.

Below *Punk styles continued into the eighties, when some punks adopted the all-black "Goth" look. This girl was photographed in Covent Garden, London.*

Heavy metal rockers

The heavy metal style was associated with motorcycle gangs and had been around since the late sixties. Most heavy metal types were male, long-haired, and clad in leather or denim. Swastikas and death's head emblems were worn for shock effect. Heavy metal music was played by very loud drum-and-guitar groups including Slayer, Metallica, Judas Priest, and Iron Maiden.

Psychedelics

Anyone wearing the swirling Op art, paisley, or psychedelic patterns of the sixties might come into this category. The term psychedelic means "mind expanding" and it originally referred to drugs such as LSD which distort perception of reality, sometimes creating hallucinations. The Bangles were one of the groups of the eighties whose jangling guitars recalled the sixties sound.

Facing page *Heavy metal fans. Their outfits include denim jackets worn with leather, badges, and studs. One fan is playing an air guitar—an imaginary guitar.*

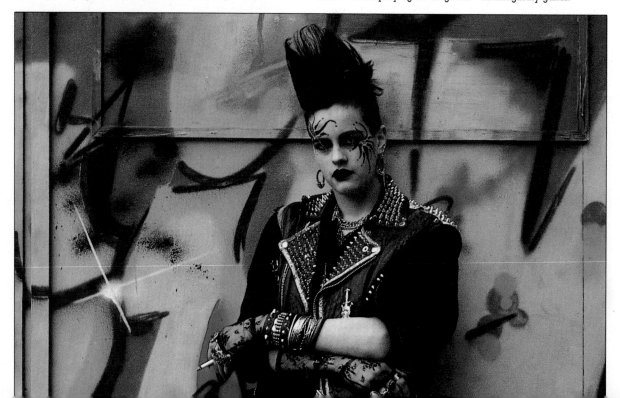

DESIGN

People became very conscious of design in the eighties, and such terms as designer label and designer stubble reflected this new awareness.

In the early eighties the trend was very much for the "high tech" or high-technology look. The idea was to celebrate the appearance of industrial buildings—oil refineries, warehouses, and factories—with their metal piping and girders. Things should look "functional," that is, be designed to reveal their practical purpose, with no frills or decoration. In the home, a shelving system might be made of plain metal racks, for example, instead of polished wood. Every new item, such as a Walkman® stereo or a pocket camera, was designed to look like a functional little "black box" or "steel box."

Above *This stereo headset is postmodernist in design. Unlike earlier "black boxes" it is made of bright, yellow plastic with trim in other colors.*

Above *The corner of this teenager's bedroom is in high-tech style with its plain, white walls and modern, tubular shelving system.*

More generally, anything suggesting sophisticated new technology might be termed high-tech. Examples included watches with the new digital face instead of old-fashioned hands on the dial; and the flat-screen TV introduced by Sony in 1982.

One personal item became something of a cult object. This was the Filofax, a portable ring binder system for filing information about work, home, or private life. The Filofax was particularly popular among ''yuppies''—another catchword of the eighties. Yuppy stands for young urban professional and the word was often used to describe a certain type of ambitious young adult. Yuppies were often very hard working, but they were also eager to enjoy the pleasures of modern society such as designer clothes and CD players.

Computer design, synthetic materials

Ever since microchips first appeared in the seventies, computer technology had been transforming everyday life. Microchips are tiny wafers of silicon smaller than a postage stamp, that can serve as the main processing unit of a computer. Microchips allowed a whole new

Below *A variety of digital watches became available in the eighties. The one on the left includes a miniature radio receiver, with headphones.*

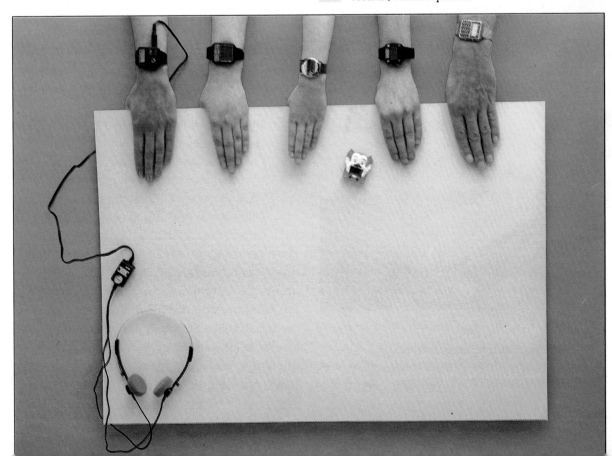

generation of computers to be built, much smaller than earlier examples, so that they could fit onto a desk top at home, at school, or in the office.

Designers in the eighties also used computers to perform very complex tasks, such as drawing "three-dimensional" images on a screen. The body of a car, a spacecraft, or a building, for example, would appear as a "wireframe" image that could then be revolved and viewed from all angles. Computers offered a wealth of other possibilities. The hit movie *Who Framed Roger Rabbit?* (1988) used computer-generated cartoons alongside human actors. Another example, TV's Max Headroom, was a brilliant creation very popular among older teenagers. He was the comic host of a TV video show, and was played by an actor in la-

Above *Computer graphics allowed designers to create complex images on the computer screen, and then bend them or revolve them in three dimensions.*

tex makeup. To make Max look like a half-human robot, images of him were mixed under computer control with background graphics that were also generated by computer. The effects were weirdly disconcerting—and hilarious.

Designers in the eighties were anxious to use new synthetic materials. One of the most remarkable creations of the time was the C5, an electric three-wheeled car launched by Clive Sinclair (the chief pioneer of home computers). The vehicle's body shell was entirely of molded polypropylene, a type of plastic, and the C5 was steered by handlebars beneath the rider's knees. The idea was to try and replace gasoline-driven cars for short trips in cities. Unfortunately, though, the C5 failed to catch on, partly because the light, synthetic body offered so little protection amid city traffic. Shortly after the launch in 1985, production was halted.

Postmodernism

The original high-tech look stressed strict, functional simplicity in design. But during the eighties another trend emerged and caught on quickly with the public. This has been called the "postmodernist" movement and it encouraged little decorative flourishes in design that are often borrowed from the past, with small areas of color and a sense of fun.

One famous example in architecture was the Public Services Building in Portland, Oregon. Completed in 1983, it was designed by American architect Michael Graves in a colorful style reminiscent of ancient Egyptian structures. Another influence was the Memphis group of furniture designers in Italy. At the Milan Furniture Fair of 1981, they produced many items in bright colors with patterns that recalled fabrics such as leopard skin which were very popular in the fifties. Ideas like these had long been considered in bad taste, but the trend con-

Above *The postmodern Public Service Building in Portland, Oregon. Colored decoration and features such as these triangular blocks help to add interest and variety to its appearance.*

tinued. Another Italian designer, Michele de Lucchi, came up with designs for everyday items such as vacuum cleaners and toasters that made them look like children's toys.

Color and fun entered department and specialty stores as designers started to challenge the functional "black box" look. Flashlights, watches, cameras, and personal stereos were now produced in brightly colored plastic as "fashion accessories." Typical colors included lilac, flamingo pink, bright yellow, and a slightly acid day-glo green. Teenagers could buy goods, such as sunglasses, sneakers, jewelry, belts, or even a Walkman, to match the colors of their favorite clothes, so that they matched from head to toe.

IMAGES OF THE EIGHTIES

Royal wedding

On July 29, 1981, Prince Charles, heir to the British throne, married Lady Diana Spencer, the shy, attractive daughter of one of Britain's aristocratic families. The wedding took place in St. Paul's Cathedral in London and 700 million television viewers all around the world watched the pomp and pageantry as the couple walked down the aisle. The young bride was wearing a billowing wedding dress of ivory silk, with an immensely long train. It gave her the look of "a fairytale princess" and contributed to the fashionable New Romantic look of the early eighties. Afterward the couple rode to Buckingham Palace in a horse-drawn carriage. They kissed on the palace balcony before an enormous, cheering crowd.

Above *The Prince and Princess of Wales on the balcony at Buckingham Palace, July 1981.*

Afghanistan

Afghanistan is a mountainous land that borders the Soviet Union. In December 1979 the Soviet Union invaded the country to support a pro-Soviet government that seemed on the brink of collapse. Civil war erupted. The Afghan government and its Soviet allies controlled the towns, while wily resistance fighters waged a fierce hit-and-run guerrilla war from the hills. The main resistance group was the Muslim Mujehadeen whose members believed that they were fighting a jihad or holy war against the enemy.

The war dragged on through the eighties. The 115,000 Soviet troops found themselves hampered by poor roads and rocky terrain, and they could not defeat the guerrilla tactics of the resistance. The war had also created a serious political rift between the United States and the Soviet Union. Eventually, Soviet leader Mikhail Gorbachev ordered a Russian withdrawal. The last Soviet troops left Afghanistan in February 1989.

Above *An Afghan rebel photographed in 1981. These tribesmen used guerrilla tactics to harrass the Soviet invaders into withdrawing in 1989.*

Disaster at Chernobyl

In April 1986 an accident struck one of the Soviet Union's nuclear power stations. The plant was at Chernobyl, about 80 miles north of the city of Kiev. One of the reactors at Chernobyl was badly damaged and a seemingly uncontrollable fire raged in its core. Clouds of radioactive material leaked into the atmosphere and were carried by winds over places as far away as Norway, Sweden, Finland, and Great Britain. The Soviet Union had to evacuate the entire area around the plant itself, and needed expert help from other countries to control the fire. Though only two people were reported killed it was certain that more would eventually die from radiation poisoning. The disaster caused many more people to question the safety of nuclear power as a source of energy.

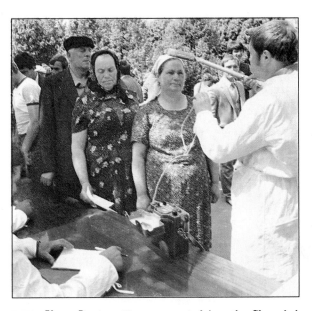

Above *Russian citizens evacuated from the Chernobyl area are checked for radiation levels after the 1986 nuclear accident.*

Above *The seventh space shuttle is launched from Kennedy Space Center in June 1983 with Dr. Sally Ride on board.*

Space shuttle

America's space shuttle made its maiden flight on April 12, 1981. The importance of the craft was the winged orbiter, about the size of an airliner. Launched by booster rockets, the orbiter was designed to carry payloads such as satellites into orbit, then glide back to Earth to be used again.

Many successful flights were made, and among the crews was Sally Ride, America's first woman in space. In January 1986, however, disaster struck. Only a few seconds after the 25th shuttle mission was launched a fatal explosion destroyed the spacecraft in midair before thousands of spectators. All seven people on board died instantly. The crew included a high school teacher, Christa McAuliffe, who had been chosen as the first private citizen to fly in a shuttle. Shuttle flights began again in 1988; by that time the Soviet Union was setting new records for space endurance.

Lebanon

Lebanon was one of the world's most troubled regions. The country lies in the politically troubled area at the eastern end of the Mediterranean, bordering Israel to the south. As a result of Arab-Israeli fighting a large number of Palestinian refugees and guerrillas entered the country during the seventies. Lebanon has its own rich mix of principal peoples, including three sects of Muslims and a strong Christian element. The new Palestinian arrivals contributed to mounting rivalries that erupted in almost permanent civil war.

By 1980, 33 private armies or militias were fighting for control. Syria invaded the country to try and help the Muslims; the Israelis invaded to try and drive out Palestinian guerrillas. A United Nations peace-keeping force tried but failed to keep order. Nothing seemed capable of ending the strife. Gunfire, bombings, kidnappings, and assassinations continued throughout the eighties.

One of the techniques of the militias was to seize foreign hostages, often Americans or Europeans. Terry Waite, a special representative of the Archbishop of Canterbury of England, was skilled at negotiating the release of such hostages, but in 1987 he was himself kidnapped and held hostage.

War in the Falklands

The bleak little island group of the Falklands lies about 500 miles east of the mainland of South America. The Falklands have been a British colony since 1833, and the inhabitants are mostly of British descent. However, Argentina has long laid claim to the islands, and prospects of valuable oil deposits offshore made the dispute worse. In April 1982 the Argentinians made a surprise attack on the Falklands and put them under military occupation. In reply, Mrs. Thatcher sent a British task force to win them back. A short, bloody war followed in which over a thousand British and Ar-

gentinian servicemen lost their lives. The result was a British victory, and afterward Britain continued to keep a garrison of some 4,000 troops on the island.

Above *The Argentinian cruiser General Belgrano is sunk by a British ship in May 1982, during the first major encounter of the Falklands War.*

Below *Damage from Israeli bombings in West Beirut, 1982. The Israelis mounted a full-scale invasion in that year and did not leave until 1985.*

Above *Victims of drought in Ethiopia. TV showed the world the thousands of starving refugees that took shelter in relief camps.*

Famine in Ethiopia

Terrible famine plagued Ethiopia in the eighties. This country of poor herdsmen and farmers in East Africa experienced its longest-running drought of recent times. The government was also involved in a long civil war and devoted much of its energy and resources to the fighting. The result was hunger on a horrific scale. By mid-1985 more than 250,000 people had died of starvation. Thousands of refugees took shelter at famine relief camps and heart-wrenching pictures of their suffering were seen on TV screens all around the world. In response, a massive international relief operation was mounted. The famine also stirred the consciences of rock music stars who donated their time and talent to make the charity record *Do They Know It's Christmas?* and took part in the Live Aid concert held on July 13, 1985.

Mount St. Helens volcano

Mount St. Helens is a volcano in the Cascade Mountain Range of southwestern Washington. It had been dormant, or inactive, since 1857. On March 27, 1980, however, the earth started trembling in the area around it. Steam blasts were observed coming from the top, and a swelling started to appear on the north flank. Then came the eruption. On the clear sunny morning of May 18, a tremendous series of explosions occurred. They sent a column of ash shooting up more than 12 miles into the air, producing fallout that spread for more than 900 miles. As molten lava spilled down the sides, catastrophic mudflows and floods were generated by the rapid melting of snow and ice. The blast from the volcano was thought to be 500 times as powerful as the Hiroshima atomic bomb, and was followed by lesser eruptions in the weeks that followed. Although it was an exciting opportunity for scientists, the eruption left 57 people missing or dead.

Solidarity in Poland

Food shortages and other problems led to widespread unrest in Poland. In 1980 there was a wave of workers' strikes that gave birth to the Solidarity movement. This was the first independent trade union in Eastern Europe and it threatened vast changes in Polish society. For 16 months Solidarity flourished. Then the country's new leader, General Jaruzelski, acted firmly against the union. He declared martial law, ordered mass arrests, and banned Solidarity. The situation had eased by the end of 1983 but workers and government remained suspicious of one another. Lech Walesa, leader of Solidarity, was given the Nobel Peace Prize for 1983, in tribute to his union's stand. Toward the end of the decade, the Polish government was showing signs of greater tolerance toward Solidarity and of allowing them to play a greater part in the political process. Finally, in 1989 a majority of Solidarity legislators was elected to the Polish national assembly.

Above *Mount St. Helens during the great volcanic eruption of 1980. By the end of the decade wildlife was returning to the area.*

Below *Slogans and striking workers at the Lenin shipyard in Gdansk, Poland, a center of the Solidarity movement in 1980.*

Reagan and Thatcher

The two figures who dominated politics in the United States and Britain were President Ronald Reagan and Prime Minister Margaret Thatcher. Reagan and Thatcher pursued conservative policies at home. Both were also firmly anticommunist, and they increased spending on defense. In 1983 President Reagan sent Marines into the Caribbean island of Grenada to stop a communist takeover, and he also urged American support for *Contra* guerrillas fighting the left-wing Sandinista government of Nicaragua in Central America.

President Reagan and Prime Minister Thatcher were both plagued by a severe recession, or slump in world trade, during the early years of the eighties. Unemployment in both countries was then very high. By the mid-eighties, however, there were definite signs of economic recovery.

Below *Friends President Ronald Reagan and Prime Minister Margaret Thatcher inspect a model of the space shuttle.*

Gorbachev

In March 1985 a new leader came to power in the Soviet Union. His name is Mikhail Gorbachev and at the age of 54 he was much younger than his predecessors. Gorbachev was also eager to reform the Soviet system that, he believed, had failed to keep pace with developments in the modern world. Gorbachev called for greater democracy: voters should be given a real choice of candidates in elections. He called for a new spirit of *glasnost*, or openness, in public life. And he also called for *perestroika*, or reconstruction, in the economy and in society as a whole. Gorbachev traveled widely abroad and his reforming spirit helped to ease tensions between East and West. In December 1987 he and President Reagan signed a major new arms control agreement. This treaty covered Intermediate Range Nuclear Forces (INF); that is, nuclear weapons of medium range. This new and exciting dialogue between the superpowers helped to ease the fears of many about a nuclear war.

Above *Soviet leader Mikhail Gorbachev talks to car-factory workers in Moscow about reforming Soviet industry and increasing production.*

The Green Movement

Pressure groups, like Greenpeace and Friends of the Earth, were active in many parts of the world during the eighties. Through daring protests they raised conservation issues to public attention and helped to put care of the environment high on the political agenda. Many governments, especially in Europe, are now eager to show they are actively promoting policies that help to conserve rain forests, protect the atmosphere, combat acid rain, and preserve wildlife in danger of extinction. It is yet to be seen how effective these policies will prove to be.

Left *Members of Greenpeace protest against the pollution of the oceans by the dumping of chemical and nuclear waste.*

GLOSSARY

Aerobics A system of physical exercise aiming to speed up breathing and get the blood circulating.

AIDS (Acquired Immune Deficiency Syndrome) A lethal virus disease that spread rapidly throughout the world in the mid-eighties. It can be transmitted by sexual intercourse, or through the mingling of one person's blood with another (as may happen when heroin addicts share a needle).

Born-again Christians People who have experienced an intense exultation, or a feeling of being reborn, when converted or reconverted to Christianity.

Cable TV A television system in which programs are sent to receivers by cable. It is only for subscribers; that is, people who pay for the system.

Cocaine A very strong, addictive stimulant drug derived from the South American coca plant. It usually appears in the form of a white powder. In the eighties an even more dangerous new form of cocaine appeared—"crack." Crack use spread especially among unemployed teenagers. Overdose deaths sometimes occurred among users, who were also prone to intense depression when off the drug.

Communism A political theory aiming to establish a society in which major enterprises such as factories, mines, farms, and stores are owned by all citizens rather than specific individuals or groups of people. In practice, Communist societies have tended to create powerful state authorities that control the nation's enterprises.

Condom A thin, rubber sheath that covers the penis during sexual intercourse, providing some protection from venereal and other diseases such as AIDS, as well as preventing conception.

Conservative A word to describe people who wish to hold on to established customs and values. People described as conservative are generally cautious of any change, unless the change is a return to earlier practices.

Contraceptive Any device used to prevent an unwanted pregnancy.

Contras Right-wing guerrillas in Nicaragua, campaigning to overthrow the elected, left-wing government.

Feminism The movement aiming to win full rights and respect for women in society, and to celebrate the unique qualities of the female sex.

Glasnost A policy of openness introduced by Mikhail Gorbachev in the Soviet Union. It permitted greater freedom of discussion in the media, for example.

Heroin A dangerous and highly addictive drug derived from morphine. It is basically narcotic; that is, it slows down the body's system. An overdose can result in coma or death.

High-tech The high-technology design style of the early eighties. It was originally based on the functional look of industrial buildings, but might include anything that suggested advanced, modern technology.

Homosexual (or gay) Someone who is sexually attracted to members of the same sex.

Laser A device using the energy of intensely pure light. The first lasers appeared in the sixties, and by the eighties they were performing a variety of tasks, from eye surgery to use in compact disc players.

Microchip A tiny chip of silicon containing the circuits for a computer.

Militia An army formed among private citizens (as distinct from professional soldiers).

MTV (Music Television) The rock-music video channel on cable TV.

Perestroika The policy introduced by Mikhail Gorbachev to try to reform and rebuild society in the Soviet Union. *Perestroika* is a Russian word meaning "reconstruction."

Permissiveness A view of life that holds that people should be allowed to do as they please, with as little interference as possible.

Postmodernism A design style that brought back a taste for color, decoration, and fun after the severe, functional look of the strict "modernist" approach.

Radioactivity The emission of waves or particles after a nuclear reaction occurs. A nuclear explosion or the leakage of material from a nuclear plant can cause radiation sickness. Symptoms range from headache and nausea to cancer and death.

Recession A slowing down of business activity and the economy.

Synthesizer A machine with a keyboard producing music through electronic circuits.

Unemployment The condition of being out of work. Unemployment was at its worst in the mid-eighties when there were over 11 million people out of work in the United States and some 3 million in Britain.

Video cassette recorder (VCR) An electronic apparatus that allows video tapes to be shown on a television screen, and to record television programs on tape.

Yuppies Short for "young urban professionals"; the term was used to describe young adults working in well-paid jobs who were eager both for success and material goods.

FURTHER READING

At the time of writing very little has been published on the eighties as a decade. However, the following books provide useful background reading:

Chronicle of the 20th Century (Chronicle Pub., 1987)

The World Almanac and Book of Facts (New Enterprises Association, 1988)

All Grown Up and No Place to Go, David Elkind (Addison-Wesley, 1984)

The Postponed Generation, Susan Littwin (William Morrow, 1986)

Rock Stars, Timothy White (Stuart, Tabori & Chang, 1984)

The Young People's Yellow Pages, Alvin Rosenbaum (Putnam, 1983)

Smart Choices, Nancy & Robert Kolodny, and Thomas Bratter (Little, Brown, 1986)

Additionally, the following offer a humorous view of a teenager's life in the early eighties:

The Secret Diary of Adrian Mole, Aged 13¾, Sue Townsend (Avon, 1987)

The Growing Pains of Adrian Mole, Sue Townsend (Avon, 1987)

Picture Acknowledgments

Architectural Association 37; Barnaby's Picture Library 35t; Daily Telegraph Colour Library (Andrew McKim) 36; DHSS 27; Greenpeace/Walker 45b; Hutchison Library 6, 32; Kobal Collection *cover, lower left*, 20, 21; Photri 7, 19, 25, 28, 38, 40, 43b, 44, 45t; Redferns 13, 14, 15; Rex Features *cover, right*, 10b, 16, 33; TOPHAM *cover, upper left*, 4, 5, 8, 9, 11, 12, 17t, 17b, 18, 22l, 22r, 23, 24, 26t, 26b, 29, 31, 34, 35b, 39t, 39b, 41t, 41b, 42; Courtesy The U.S. Geological Survey 43t; Wayland 10t, 30t, 30b.

INDEX